SLOTH LIFE

DON'T HURRY, BE HAPPY

summersdale

SLOTH LIFE

An Hachette UK Company
www.hachette.co.uk

Summersdale Publishers Ltd
Part of Octopus Publishing Group Limited
Carmelite House
50 Victoria Embankment
LONDON
EC4Y 0DZ
UK

www.summersdale.com

Printed and bound in China

ISBN: 978-1-78685-554-1

Substantial discounts on bulk quantities of Summersdale books are available to corporations, professional associations and other organisations. For details contact general enquiries: telephone: +44 (0) 1243 771107 or email: enquiries@summersdale.com.

To..

From......................................

The sloth life
chose me.

Note to self:

be 100%
fabulous today.

Move along,
slothing
to see here⭐

BE-LEAF IN YOURSELF.

Sun, sea, sand...
Call me
**David
Hassel-sloth.**

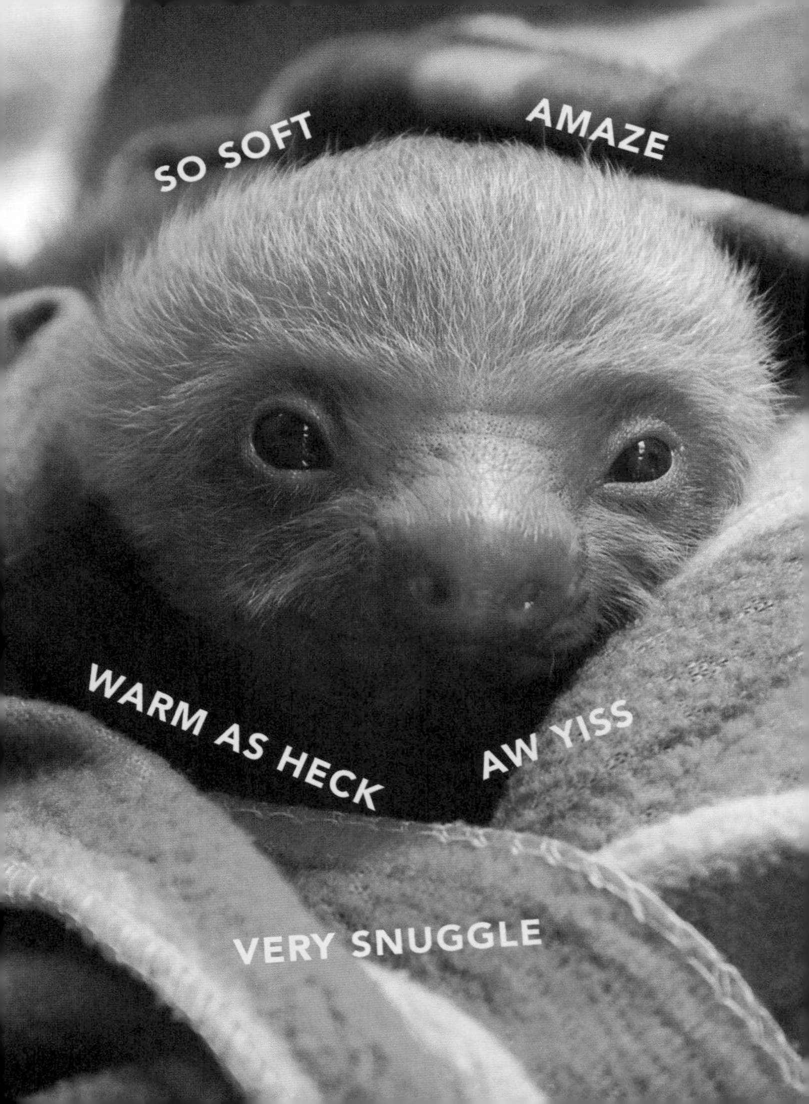
SO SOFT
AMAZE
WARM AS HECK
AW YISS
VERY SNUGGLE

AND HERE IS A
SLOTH IN ITS
DESIRED
HABITAT.

Sloth mode:

I'm toe-tally AWESOME.

Be more sloth!

Ain't no
Snuggle like a
soft sloth
Snuggle.★

BIG
SPOON

LITTLE
SPOON

I'D
RATHER
BE
SLEEPING ⭐

#BFF

You miss 100%
of the naps you
don't take.

UPWARD-
FACING
SLOTH.

The relaxing art of

SLOGA.

Nap
all day,
sleep
all night,
party
never ⭐

Dream BIG.

Live ★

Laugh ★

Sloth ★

TO DO:
RELAX.

Live slow,
die whenever.✦

Be the sloth
you wish to see
in the world.

Feeling
PHILOSLOTHICAL.

WHO RUN
THE WORLD?
NOT ME.
I DON'T KNOW
HOW TO RUN.

I SLEEP,
THEREFORE
I SLOTH.

Sloth
is not
a sin.

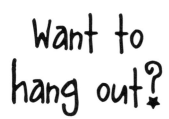

Want to
hang out?

I'M KIND OF A BIG DEAL.

I'm not lazy,
I'm just
really good at

DOING
NOTHING.

Turn that frown upside down.

IF AT FIRST YOU DON'T SUCCEED, HAVE A NAP.

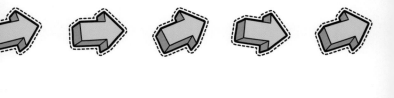

STILL LAPPING EVERYONE ON THE COUCH.★

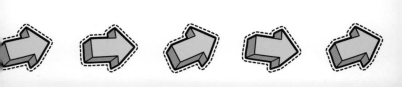

Born to be
MILD.⭐

No naps,
no glory

Tomorrow
I'll quit
PROCRASTINATING.★

We've never had a problem we couldn't HUG OUT.

p.50 – photo © AKKHARAT JARUSILAWONG/Shutterstock.com; leaves Virina/Shutterstock.com

p.52 – leaves © daisybee/Shutterstock.com

p.53 – photo © Parkol/Shutterstock.com; chain © EgudinKa/Shutterstock.com; gold leaf © mirrelley/Shutterstock.com

p.54 – photo © worldswildlifewonders/Shutterstock.com; tropical stickers © Martyshova Maria/Shutterstock.com

p.56 – leaves © daisybee/Shutterstock.com

p.57 – photo © Jordan Adkins/Shutterstock.com; flowers © nosik/Shutterstock.com

p.58 – photo © Treviso Photography/Shutterstock.com

p.58-59 – triangles © Marianne Thompson

p.61 – photo © Evelyn Dutra/Shutterstock.com; crown © Annykos/Shutterstock.com

p.62 – photo © Janossy Gergely/Shutterstock.com

p.63 – leaves © Inna Moreva/Shutterstock.com

p.64 – tropical illustration © Inna Moreva/Shutterstock.com

p.65 – photo © Kristel Segeren/Shutterstock.com

p.66 – photo © Zoltan Tarlacz/Shutterstock.com; hanging moon and stars © Dzm1try/Shutterstock.com

p.68 – wings © anpannan/Shutterstock.com

p.69 – photo © Nacho Such/Shutterstock.com

p.70 – snail © SlyBrowney/Shutterstock.com

p.70-71 – photo © Davydele/Shutterstock.com

p.73 – photo © Jordan Adkin/Shutterstock.com; pizza © Mochipet/Shutterstock.com

p.74 – photo © Parkol/Shutterstock.com

p.75 – leaves © Inna Moreva/Shutterstock.com

p.76 – flowers © Virina/Shutterstock.com

p.77 – photo © Sarine Arslanian/Shutterstock.com; flower © Virina/Shutterstock.com

p.78-79 – photo © Bildagentur Zoonar GmbH/Shutterstock.com; leaf © Virina/Shutterstock.com

p.81 – photo © Kristel Segeren/Shutterstock.com

p.82 – photo © Matthew W Keefe/Shutterstock.com; foam hand © Luchenko Yana/Shutterstock.com

p.83 – arrows © Martyshova Maria/Shutterstock.com

p.85 – photo © Nina B/Shutterstock.com; sticker hearts © zizi_mentos /Shutterstock.com; plain hearts © Colorlife/Shutterstock.com

p.86 – photo © worldswildlifewonders/Shutterstock.com

p.86-87 – bunting © mirrelley/Shutterstock.com

p.87 – crown © notbad/Shutterstock.com

p.88-89 – photo © Nacho Such/Shutterstock.com

p.89 – flower © Virina/Shutterstock.com

p.90 – photo © Alastair Munro/Shutterstock.com; peace © Lelene/Shutterstock.com

p.91 – triangles © Marianne Thompson

p.92-93 – photo © Kobby Dagan/Shutterstock.com; stars © Martyshova Maria/Shutterstock.com

p.96 – hanging sloth © littleWhale/Shutterstock.com

If you're interested in
finding out more about our
books, find us on Facebook at
Summersdale Publishers
and follow us on Twitter at
@Summersdale.

www.summersdale.com